TARANTULAS

WEIRD PETS

Lynn M. Stone

Rourke Publishing LLC
Vero Beach, Florida 32964

www.rourkepublishing.com

PHOTO CREDITS:
All photos © Lynn M. Stone

EDITORIAL SERVICES:
Pamela Schroeder

Library of Congress Cataloging-in-Publication Data

Stone, Lynn M.
      Tarantulas / Lynn M. Stone
          p. cm—(Weird Pets)
      ISBN 1-58952-041-6
        1.Tarantulas as pets—Juvenile literature [1. Tarantulas as pets.
      2. Spiders. 3. Pets.] I. Title.

SF459.T37 S78 2001
639.7—dc21   00-054283

Printed in the USA

TABLE OF CONTENTS

TARANTULAS

Spiders are scary to many people. The bigger the spider, the scarier it seems to be!

Other people like spiders. Some of these people keep the biggest and hairiest spiders as pets!

People in North and Central America call these big, hairy spiders "tarantulas."

A pet red-kneed tarantula crawls on its owner's hand.

There are over 800 **species**, or kinds, of tarantulas. About 30 species live in North America, most of them in the dry Southwest.

The word *tarantula* came from Italy. There are no tarantulas in Italy or anywhere else in Europe! However, in Taranto, Italy, people long ago called a kind of wolf spider "tarantula."

An Indian tree spider resting on a pile of leaves

Tarantulas are in a different family of spiders than wolf spiders. Wolf spiders live in North America. Like tarantulas, they're hairy. But tarantulas are *really* big. Some of them are the size of a man's hand.

Like all spiders, tarantulas have eight legs. They also have eight bright little eyes, but tarantulas hunt mostly by their sense of touch.

The hairy legs of a tarantula allow it to crawl on almost any surface, even glass.

Tarantulas are meat eaters, or **carnivores**. They live on insect **prey**. The biggest tarantulas eat bigger prey—frogs, lizards, and small snakes. The bird-eating tarantula's name tells you about what it eats.

Many people fear tarantulas because of their **venom**. Venom is any poison that an animal makes. Tarantulas and other venomous animals use venom to kill prey.

A giant white-kneed tarantula (right) rests by its old skin, or molt.

With a lid and air holes added, an old aquarium can be made into a tarantula cage.

A tarantula can be placed in a plastic bowl while its cage is cleaned.

People with pet tarantulas are careful about which species they have. A bite from the most poisonous tarantula won't kill a healthy person. However, tarantula bites hurt. And any animal bite may carry germs.

Some tarantulas can throw hairs from their back at anything that frightens them. The hairs don't grow back until the tarantula sheds, or **molts**, its old skin. Until then, the tarantula may have a bald spot on its body.

Crawling on a sweatshirt, a pet tarantula shows the bald spot left from where it threw hairs.

rnamental
e-Spider

Emperor Scorpion
Central Africa

Tarantula

TARANTULAS: PET FRIENDLY?

Tarantulas are fuzzy, all right, but they're not warm or cuddly. In fact, some experts say that tarantula owners should never handle their pets. Unlike a dog, a tarantula will never look forward to its owner's touch.

Pet tarantulas take up little space. Some species, like those from dry places, are easy to care for. Some species are very colorful.

Tarantula owners are careful because tarantulas can be hurt easily if they're dropped.

Tarantulas can be fun to watch. They hunt, hide, spin webs, run around, and grow when they molt.

Tarantula owners who hold their pets may get a rash from tarantula hairs. Owners also risk having the tiny hairs end up in their eyes. They could also be bitten. Each species is different. Some, like the rose-hair, are calm. Others are quick to bite.

A rose-hair tarantula prepares to grab a cricket for dinner.

CARING FOR A TARANTULA

Someone who wants a tarantula should talk to a person who knows tarantulas well. A tarantula buyer should read about tarantula care and ask questions.

Tarantulas need a cage with good air flow. Tarantulas can't be kept too hot or too cold. They depend upon their owners for food and water, too. Each kind of tarantula has different needs. Tree species, for example, need a branch to climb on.

Tarantulas that burrow need loose soil in their cages.

FINDING A TARANTULA

Finding a tarantula is not hard. Many pet shops sell tarantulas. Dealers sell tarantulas on-line. Tarantulas are also for sale at some pet shows.

It is important to know if your tarantula is male or female. Males live only a few months. Females may live for years.

Common species cost about $15. Rare tarantulas can cost hundreds of dollars.

GLOSSARY

carnivore (KAR neh vor) — a meat-eating animal, such as a lion

molt (MOWLT) — to shed hair, skin, feathers, or other outer layer

prey (PRAY) — an animal that is hunted by another animal
for food

species (SPEE sheez) — within a group of closely related
animals, such as tarantulas, one certain type (*rose-hair* tarantula)

venom (VEN em) — a poison made by some animals, and usually
used to kill prey

INDEX

Further Reading

Martin, Louise. *Tarantulas* Rourke Publishing, 1988

Websites To Visit

• www.tarantulaplanet.org   • www.stshq.org

About The Author

Lynn Stone is the author of over 400 children's books. He is a talented natural history photographer as well. Lynn, a former teacher, travels worldwide to photograph wildlife in their natural habitat.